RICH

FAMOUS

in Starvation Lake

by Gloria Whelan
illustrated by Lynne Cravath

For Kathy
G.W.

To Sigi
L.C.

Library of Congress Cataloging-in-Publication Data
Whelan, Gloria.
Rich and famous in Starvation Lake / by Gloria Whelan ; illustrated by
Lynne Cravath.
  p.   cm. — (Road to reading. Mile 5)
Summary: During a long, snowy winter, the fourth grade boys and girls at
Starvation Lake Elementary School have a contest to see who can raise the most
money to help pay for a class trip.
ISBN 0-307-26511-0 (pbk.) — ISBN 0-307-46511-X (GB)
[1. Schools—Fiction. 2. Contests—Fiction. 3. Winter—Fiction. 4. Friendship—
Fiction.] I. Cravath, Lynne Woodcock, ill. II. Title. III. Series.

PZ7.W5718 Ri 2001
[Fic]—dc21   00-061002

A GOLDEN BOOK • New York

Golden Books Publishing Company, Inc. New York, New York 10106

Text © 2001 Gloria Whelan. Illustrations © 2001 Golden Books
Publishing Company, Inc. All rights reserved. No part of this book
may be copied or reproduced without written permission from the
publisher. A GOLDEN BOOK®, GOLDEN BOOKS®, G DESIGN®,
and SHIELD DESIGN™ are trademarks of Golden Books
Publishing Company, Inc.

ISBN: 0-307-26511-0 (pbk)
ISBN: 0-307-46511-X (GB)

10   9   8   7   6   5   4   3   2   1

Contents

1
The Contest

It was another perfectly awful day in Starvation Lake. Stacey Ward stood outside her house watching the school bus lumber through the snow. It had been snowing for twenty-three days straight. Stacey was getting sick of all that white.

Yesterday, Weird Mom had filled the garden sprayer with water and vegetable dye. She started spraying the snow around the house grass-green.

Stacey knew how her mom felt. She had bought ten cents' worth of grass seed at the feed store and scooped some dirt out of one of her mom's plants. Now she had a nice little lawn growing in a saucer.

The school bus ground to a stop. The door swung open, letting in a whirlwind of snow. Stacey climbed onto the bus.

"Morning, Stacey," Elvera said. Elvera was the bus driver. She always wore her husband's hunting cap, the ear flaps tied down under her chin. That way she didn't have to listen to all the yelling in the bus.

"Tell your dad he'd better stop by our house this week," Elvera said. "If he doesn't, my husband and I are going to start coming to your house to use the bathroom."

Stacey's dad was a plumber. He was tall and so thin, people said he could crawl into a pipe to fix it. This time of year, he never picked up the phone. He never listened to the messages on the answering machine. They all said the same thing:

"Get right over here! Our pipes are frozen."

Stacey shook off the snow. She flopped down on the seat by Theresa Bloncheck. Theresa put away her notebook. She was writing a novel about California. In her story, it was always warm and the sun was always shining. Even at night.

"Did you think of any ideas?" asked Theresa. The fourth grade was having a contest between the boys and girls to see who could raise more money for a winter overnight at the ecology camp. School funds would pay for the overnight, but the class had to contribute, too.

Stacey put her purple nail polish on the bus's heater to thaw. "No ideas yet, but yesterday I heard Kevin and Mark whispering in the cafeteria. They must be up to something. The boys are going to win if we don't think of something fast."

When the bus pulled up at the trailer park, everyone quieted down. There was going to be a new girl in the fourth grade. Her name was Dawn Zonder.

Stacey said, "I heard the school social worker talking to Ms. LaForest." Ms. LaForest was their fourth-grade teacher. "The social worker said, 'Dawn is going through a difficult time. She'll need a lot of sympathy and understanding.'"

"I think her mom is in a hospital down-state waiting for a new heart," Theresa said. "Dawn came up here to stay with her grandmother so her dad could be with her mother."

Everyone watched Dawn climb onto the bus. She was carrying a stuffed moose. It was nearly as big as she was.

"I thought we weren't supposed to take stuffed animals to school," Theresa said.

Stacey said, "I think that's part of the sympathy and understanding."

Dawn gave the window seat to her moose and huddled next to it. Stacey wanted to say something friendly to her, but Dawn kept her head down. She wouldn't look at anyone.

Baylor Proust's mother was waiting at the bus stop in the snow. The minute she spotted the bus, she ran inside to get Baylor. Mrs. Proust wouldn't let Baylor wait outside.

Baylor was so wrapped up in heavy clothes, he could hardly climb aboard. "How you feeling, Baylor?" Elvera asked. She didn't bother to lift her ear flaps for the answer. It was always the same.

"Not very well." Baylor usually had a cold or the flu. Or there was something wrong with one or the other end of his digestive system. No one ever remembered him saying he felt good.

The students put up with Baylor and all his complaints, but he didn't have a lot of friends. The seat next to Baylor usually stayed empty. He said he didn't care if no one sat next to him. It just meant he wouldn't get their germs.

The last stop before the school was the Ellenbergers' Happy Endings Funeral Home. Mark Ellenberger hopped on board. Everything about Mark was neat. He was wearing a white shirt and a tie.

"He looks like he's in training to take over his dad's business," Stacey whispered to Theresa.

Mark flung himself onto the seat next to Marvin Mallow, the coolest boy in class. Stacey heard Mark ask, "Did you bring your money?"

Stacey groaned. "They *have* got a plan to raise money," she said to Theresa. "We've got to get started."

The school bus rolled into the parking lot of the Starvation Lake Elementary School. "Okay," Elvera called out. "Rats off the ship. If I find any trash left behind on my bus, you'll all be walking home."

2
Boys Against Girls

The principal, Mr. Chickering, stood at the entrance to the school. He was nagging the kids as they trudged up the steps. "Get the snow off those boots before you come in."

There was a little bit more of Mr. Chickering than there needed to be. Every day, his wife packed him vegetables with yogurt dip and two kinds of fruit for lunch, but he couldn't stay out of the school cafeteria. He walked up and down between the tables. If the students didn't watch out, he'd sneak one of their chicken wings or a piece of their burrito.

Once he snatched a whole slice of pizza from Kevin Brown. Kevin said he'd get his parents to sue if Mr. Chickering didn't buy him another slice. Both of Kevin's parents were lawyers.

Lockers were opened and a lot of stuff fell out—books and rotten apples and dried-up peanut-butter sandwiches and a mitten with no mate and papers that were supposed to go home because they had a bad grade on them.

Stacey walked into the fourth-grade classroom. The first thing she did was check out what Ms. LaForest was wearing. Ms. LaForest was the best-dressed teacher in the school. Today she had on a pleated skirt held together with a big safety pin, black tights, and a black turtleneck sweater. But she was crying again.

Stacey wasn't surprised. It happened every time the lesson plan called for the computer. On the first day of the year, the school board had plopped the computer down in the classroom like it was a pencil sharpener or an eraser. They expected teachers to know all about computers. Ms. LaForest didn't.

Tommy Kewaysaw hurried up to help Ms. LaForest. The casino where Tommy's parents worked had lots of computers in its offices. Tommy was a whiz.

Carefully wiping her eyes so her mascara wouldn't run, Ms. LaForest said, "I don't know what happened. It just died."

Tommy played with the mouse and pushed the Escape button. The computer came alive again. Just then Mr. Chickering's voice came booming over the loudspeaker.

"Moses on the mountain," Bethany Conway whispered to Stacey. Bethany's father was a minister. She knew the Bible, chapter and verse.

"Good morning, ladies and gentlemen. The temperature is three degrees. Lunch today will be tortillas, refried beans, and tomato salsa." Just a few weeks ago, Mary Hawley, the school cook, had been learning French cuisine. Her latest interest was Tex-Mex cooking.

Mr. Chickering went on. "There will be outdoor recess today." Groans. "I want to congratulate the fourth grade. They're helping to raise money toward a winter overnight at the ecology camp. And now for *The Pledge of Allegiance*."

After the Pledge, the class checked for E-mail on the computer. There was a long one from their E-mail pals in Iceland. It described all the snow in Iceland. The kids sent a message back, describing all the snow in Starvation Lake.

Ms. LaForest opened her lesson plan. She asked who had completed the poetry assignment. Only Bethany's hand went up. No one was surprised. She wrote a poem every day of her life.

Bethany stood in front of the class. Stacey sighed when she saw Bethany's dress. It had lace on the collar and a big bow tied in the back. Bethany's mother made her clothes. Weird Mom hadn't emptied the laundry hamper in weeks. All Stacey had to wear were jeans and a T-shirt she'd washed herself.

Still, Bethany's mom probably didn't sit down with her to watch *Dracula* like

Weird Mom had done with Stacey last Saturday night. Weird Mom had even served tomato juice during the video.

Bethany cleared her throat and recited in a clear, loud voice:

Moon Shadows

It's dark and snowy
And very blowy.
On the hill
Are shadows still.
The owl will fly,
The mouse will die.
Nothing left
But a pitiful wail
And a wiggling tail.

"Bethany," Ms. LaForest sighed, "your

poems start so nicely, but their endings are always so sad."

"Life is sad," Bethany said with a big smile.

The rest of the morning flew by. Stacey tried to think of a fund-raising idea during math, but Ms. LaForest kept interrupting with questions and stuff.

When recess came, the snow was blowing so hard it was impossible to see across the schoolyard. Trying to keep warm, the boys huddled together in one cluster and the girls in another. If they stood still, they got covered with snow. When they talked, little puffs came out of their mouths. The puffs were like the word balloons in comic strips.

Stacey and Mark were the last ones through the door. Stacey was trying to find

out from Mark how the boys were going to raise their money.

"Have you got something to sell, or what?" she asked.

"Whatever it is, we'll make more than you," Mark said. He walked over to a huddle of boys.

At lunch the day before, the boys had decided on their fund-raising project. At first they wanted to have a car wash. But Kevin pointed out the snow and water would probably freeze the car doors shut. Then Mark came up with an idea that wasn't exactly a regular fund-raiser. He promised, "Anyone who gives fifty cents gets a peek into the preparation room."

The preparation room was in his father's funeral home. None of them had ever actually been in a funeral home before. The boys had all brought money today to give Mark.

"There's gotta be a dead person there," Kevin said. He wasn't giving fifty cents to look at equipment.

"Sure. What did you think? Dad goes to the Hole in the Wall on Saturday mornings for the men's coffee club. Only this Saturday might not work because no one's dead. I've got my eye on a couple of people, though. Mrs. Sackrider looks awful and Mr. Doppling's been going to the doctor every week."

Mark turned to Baylor. "You've got to pay, too." Baylor looked paler than usual. All the boys were looking at him. He reluctantly dug into his pocket and stuck out his hand with two quarters in it.

"How do I know those quarters haven't

got germs on them?" Mark teased. He took the fifty cents. The other boys gave Mark their coins. He counted the money.

"We raised six dollars and fifty cents so far," Kevin called to the girls.

Stacey turned to the rest of the girls. "I wish we could figure out how the boys are raising their money."

"They won't tell," Theresa said. "How are *we* going to raise our money?"

"We have bake sales at the church," Bethany told them.

"Who knows how to bake?" Stacey looked around. Everyone was quiet.

Dawn was standing off by herself, clutching her moose. She sort of whispered, "I can make candy."

The girls were startled to hear Dawn speak.

"We could sell the candy at Blodget's Supermarket," Bethany said. "That's where the church sells their baked goods. They put a table inside the entrance and let you put your stuff on it."

Theresa asked, "Where can we make it? My mom hates it when I mess up the kitchen."

"We can do it at my house," Stacey said. Weird Mom was really relaxed about what you did in the kitchen, probably because she hardly ever went in there.

When recess was over and the lockers were full of wet mittens and melting snow from boots, Ms. LaForest said, "I have a surprise for you."

She held up a postcard from Jean and Jim Sims. The fourth grade had met them a few weeks ago when a tire fire at the junkyard closed the highway. Drivers were stranded at the school. Jean and Jim drove an eighteen-wheeler all over the country.

The card read:

Dear kids,

We just rolled into California and we're keeping our promise to send you a post-card. The weather is warm, but not so warm as the welcome we got that cold day in Starvation Lake.

Your friends,
Jean & Jim

Stacey looked out the window at the falling snow. After twenty-three days of snow, California seemed awfully far away.

3
Candy Gop

On Friday afternoon, Theresa, Dawn, and Bethany showed up at Stacey's house. A blizzard was raging, so Theresa's father had driven them in his four-wheel-drive pick-up truck. The truck was a little crowded. Dawn had brought her moose.

The girls always liked going to Stacey's. For one thing, Weird Mom made them feel welcome. For another, they never had to clean up.

Stacey let them in. "I got Jess out of the way." Jess was her seven-year-old sister. "She went with Dad to put in a new water heater for the Browns. She wants to be a plumber when she grows up."

Weird Mom beamed down at them from the top of a stepladder. "Well, girls, Stacey informs me you're making candy. Delightful. The kitchen is all yours. If you'll excuse me, I'll just get back to my painting." One wall of the living room was covered with a scene from some tropical place. The painting was a little muddled, but it wasn't hard to make out palm trees with coconuts and acres of blue sky.

Bethany said, "With all the snow outside, your picture really makes me feel warm, Mrs. Ward."

Weird Mom called down from her perch on the top of the ladder, "That's the idea. Brighten the corner where you are."

Stacey rolled her eyes, but secretly she thought she had the coolest mom in town.

Theresa and Bethany had seen the kitchen before, so they weren't surprised by the sink full of dishes. Or the sticky floor that grabbed at their shoes. Or the two cats on the counter licking the butter dish. Dawn looked a little shocked.

Stacey asked, "Dawn, did you bring the recipe?"

Dawn looked around for a clean spot to put her moose. "I don't have a recipe. I just make it. You need marshmallows and nuts and melted chocolate. You stir it all up and put it into a pan. Then you wait for it to get hard."

"Help yourselves," Stacey said. "The stuff we need has to be around here someplace. Everything else is."

Bethany began opening cupboards. "There's a bag of marshmallows here."

She took it down. "They're hard as rocks."

"Soak 'em," Stacey suggested.

Dawn screamed. The girls crowded around her. Inside one of the cupboards was a mousetrap with a leathery-looking, dried-up mouse.

"We're in luck," Theresa said. "There's a whole bag of peanuts. The mouse hardly had a chance to eat any of them."

Bethany was pulling out drawers. "I don't see any chocolate."

"You'll never find it," Stacey told her. "Weird Mom hides it on herself because she can't stop eating it. I'll go ask her where it is."

Theresa looked puzzled. "If she knows where it is, she could eat it."

Stacey explained, "That would be cheating." She checked with her mother.

When she came back, Stacey told them where to look. They found a chocolate bar hidden in the oven, another in a box of cornflakes, and one in the space behind the refrigerator.

"The chocolate bars are sort of gray," Dawn said in a small voice. No one paid attention to her.

"We need a pan to melt it in," Theresa said. She looked doubtfully at the dirty pans in the sink.

"There haven't been any clean pans in a week," Stacey said. "We'll have to wash one or just use a dirty one."

They stared at the pans for a long time. Finally Theresa picked one up. "This is the right size, but it's got some gop in it." She smelled it, then stuck her finger in and tasted it. "It's kind of sweet."

"That's all right," Stacey said. "Candy is sweet, too." She emptied all the packages of chocolate into the pan.

They took turns stirring as the chocolate heated. It smelled delicious. When it was melted, the soaked marshmallows and nuts went in. Stacey poured the whole thing out onto a platter that she had dusted off. There was nothing to do after that but lick the spoon and wait for the candy to harden.

Weird Mom came in and pronounced the result excellent. "I'm an expert on chocolate," she said, "so I know what I'm talking about."

Weird Mom let the girls paint palm trees and tigers on the living room wall. Afterward, they made popcorn and watched a video of *Little Women*. No one told them to wash their greasy fingers or pick up the popcorn that dropped behind the cushions.

"It's my second time watching *Little Women*," Stacey said.

Theresa said, "I've seen it four times."

"We show it at the church every Mother and Daughter Day," Bethany said.

Dawn hugged her moose tighter. "I've watched it about ten times," she said in her faint whisper.

Everyone was quiet. Stacey remembered Dawn's mom was in the hospital. Dawn didn't have a mother like Meg and Beth and Jo and Amy's Marmee at home. Or even one like Weird Mom.

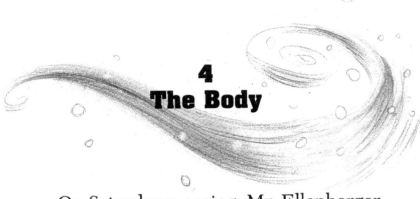

4
The Body

On Saturday morning, Mr. Ellenberger called his son into his office. Even without his black suit, Mr. Ellenberger looked plenty serious.

"Mark," he said, "I want you to hang around the funeral home for an hour or so. I'm going to the Hole in the Wall for a little coffee with the boys. Your mother had to run over to Grandma's. I don't want to leave the place alone. I brought someone in last night."

Mark's mouth dropped open. "I didn't know anyone in town died. Who was it?"

He felt a little guilty. He had told the

boys there'd probably be someone dead before long. He shouldn't have mentioned that. Maybe talking about Mrs. Sackrider and Mr. Doppling had made them die.

"No one from town, Mark. Just someone up here visiting. I'm going to take him downstate later today. Stay out of the prep room, you hear?"

"Yes, sir."

Mark watched his dad climb into the hearse. Mark always felt proud when he saw the sleek black car. It was his job to keep the hearse shined up. He washed it every weekend and vacuumed up the dead flower petals. Once a month, his mom washed and ironed the little curtains that lined the windows of the hearse.

The minute the hearse disappeared into the snow, Mark picked up the phone.

"Tommy, it's Mark. We've got one here. You need to get everyone right away. We only have an hour."

After Mark hung up, he walked quietly to the door of the prep room. He took a deep breath and eased it open an inch or two. The room was dark except for the glow from a sort of night light. A body covered with a white sheet was stretched out on the table. Hastily Mark closed the door. His heart was beating fast. His palms were sweaty. There was a tingling along the back of his neck.

The doorbell rang. It was Kevin, and just behind him were the rest of the boys who'd paid. Marvin Mallow had brought his little brother. "Hey, he's not going on our overnight," Mark said.

"Let him stay," Marvin said. "He raised

the money himself by cleaning out our turkey shed."

"Okay, but he's got to promise not to tell anyone. Wipe your feet good, everyone. Dad just got a new carpet."

The boys stamped and shuffled their feet to get rid of the snow. None of them had ever been in the Happy Endings Funeral Home before. They admired the blue carpet and the polished furniture in the reception room. A gas fire was going in the fireplace. There were lace curtains at the windows and lots of healthy green plants around.

"It looks different than I thought," Marvin said. "More cozy."

"This way." Mark led them down a long hall.

"It smells kind of funny," Tommy said.

"That's just the stuffed cabbage Mom's cooking for supper. Now you have to be totally quiet. I'm going to open the door for a minute and you all can look inside."

The boys nodded. Nobody wanted to take a *long* look at the dead person.

Mark counted, "One, two, three." He opened the door to the preparation room. The boys crowded inside. The long, thin figure lay on the table shrouded in white. They could hear one another breathing.

A minute went by. Mark was pushing them back outside the room when the figure twitched.

The boys stopped in their tracks and stared. They couldn't believe what they were seeing.

The figure slowly rose up from the table. The sheet moved with it.

"It's a ghost!" Kevin whispered.

Baylor fainted.

The boys dashed out the door. Mark slammed it shut.

"Hey!" Tommy yelled. "Baylor's still inside."

Everyone looked at Mark. "It's *your* dead person," Kevin told him.

Mark took a deep breath and yanked open the door. He dragged Baylor out. Two seconds later, they were all out on the porch, holding Baylor up. Baylor was conscious, but trembling all over. The other boys were as white as the snow. Everyone was quiet.

After a minute Mark spoke. "You guys got to pay double for that."

5
Success

Blodget's Supermarket had given the girls permission to sell their candy on Saturday afternoon. Theresa's mom drove them to the store in the animal rescue van. It smelled of dogs, but as usual, it was too cold outside to open the windows.

On either side of the parking lot, a plow was piling up snow into white mountains. The snow came down as fast as the plow pushed it out of the way. Stacey heard the familiar sound of truck wheels spinning on ice patches.

The manager, Jeff Gibbs, greeted the girls and laid down the rules. "No shouting at the customers. No pulling them over to the table. No blocking the doors so they can't get out. Good luck, and I'll be your first sale of the day." He put down a dime and tucked the candy in his pocket, planning to get rid of it. He looked like he didn't trust the girls' culinary efforts.

Bethany covered the card table with a lace cloth. Theresa had brought one of her mother's fake African violet plants. Bethany's father had exchanged two of his own dollars for coins from the church collection basket. Weird Mom had discovered a drawer full of stickers. Each wrapped piece of candy had a sticker of a fish on it. The stickers didn't exactly go with the candy, but they held the waxed paper together.

The girls gave everyone a big smile.

Bethany even helped pull out carts for the customers. But people hurried past them, eager to get farther into the warm store.

The only people who actually bought candy were people they knew—Bethany's aunt, one of the teachers from school, Theresa's grandmother. They were feeling discouraged when a traveling salesman stopped by. He'd been in the store filling the shelves with Love'em candy bars.

He winked at the girls through thick glasses. "So this is my competition. Guess I'd better try one." The salesman made a big deal out of unwrapping a piece of candy and eating it.

After a minute, he gave them a surprised look. "Hey! This stuff is good." He put down another dime and ate a second piece. "Did you really make this?"

The girls looked at one another and nodded.

"I'll take the rest of it." He began counting out dollar bills. "Who's in charge here?"

Dawn hugged her moose. Bethany looked down. Stacey pointed to their sign. "We're a committee to help raise money for the fourth-grade ecology overnight," she said. She knew not to give her name to a strange man.

"Well, it's very nice meeting you. You may hear from me again." He slipped the candy into his briefcase. Giving them a big smile, he went out the door into the snow.

Stacey counted the money. "Seven dollars and twenty cents. More than the boys made. Maybe we should make another batch."

6
The Lesson

The boys were hurrying through the snow from the funeral home to the Hole in the Wall. Mark was lagging behind. "I don't know, guys. If I tell Dad, he'll know we went into the prep room."

"You have to tell him," Kevin said. "If that dead person isn't dead, he could sue your dad for keeping him in a funeral home."

"Besides," Tommy said, "he may need a doctor instead of a funeral director."

"Sometimes our turkeys run around after they have their heads cut off," Marvin said.

Everyone was quiet after that. They wondered whether the dead person had his head on.

The boys peered through the frosty window of the restaurant. Mr. Ellenberger was having coffee with Theresa's dad, Pete Bloncheck, and Kevin's dad, Farris Brown. They were all laughing.

The boys stood outside in the falling snow until they looked like white statues. They didn't want to go inside, but it looked nice and warm in there. Finally Mark led them to the door.

Ethel Lambert owned the Hole in the Wall. She called out, "Come on in, boys, but shake off the snow first."

"Well," Mr. Brown said, "it looks like we have company."

Mark stood by his father. "Hi, Dad."

Mr. Ellenberger said, "I thought I told you to stay in the funeral home, Mark."

"It's not his fault, Mr. Ellenberger," Tommy said. "We made him come. It's sort of an emergency."

"Dad," Kevin said, "suppose someone put you in a funeral home to bury you and everything. And suppose you weren't dead. Could you sue them?"

"Well, son, you're a little young to be giving out legal advice. However, as a lawyer, I would have to admit you might have a point."

Mark cleared his throat several times. He took a deep breath. "Dad, that dead person in the prep room...he isn't."

Mr. Ellenberger stared at his son. "What do you mean, Mark?"

"I mean he isn't dead."

"Oh, I know that," Mr. Ellenberger said calmly. "That's just Sam Ward."

"Stacey's father is under the sheet?" Mark couldn't believe what he was hearing. "What's he doing there?"

Mr. Ellenberger had a wide smile on his face. "Well, Mary Hawley, your school cook, overheard you boys in the cafeteria talking about how to make a little money. And you know Mary's in the garden club with your mother. At their meeting, she passed the word on."

The boys' mouths dropped open. Mr. Ellenberger had known all along!

Mr. Bloncheck was laughing so hard, he spit out part of his coffee.

"I guess I could just have read all of you the riot act," Mr. Ellenberger chuckled. "But I figured I'd teach you a lesson

instead. Sam Ward agreed to play the corpse. He's so thin, he looks half-dead anyway."

"Baylor was really scared," Kevin said. "He fainted." Kevin turned to his dad. "Could Baylor sue Mr. Ellenberger?"

"He might, Kevin, but Mr. Ellenberger would get there first with a suit for trespassing."

"I guess the joke is on us," Mark said. "It sure looked like a real ghost."

"Tell you what I'll do, boys. I'll give you a ride back to the funeral home in the hearse and you can talk to the ghost."

The boys looked at one another. It was something special to ride in a hearse. But they weren't eager to go back to the funeral home and whatever was under that sheet—even if it was just Mr. Ward.

When he saw them hesitate, Mr. Ellenberger shooed them all outside and into the hearse. "Two boys in front and the rest of you in the back." Baylor looked like he was going to be sick. "Better sit in front with me, Baylor."

Mr. Ellenberger marched the reluctant boys to the prep room. Sam Ward was sitting up on the table, the sheet around his shoulders like a cape. "Say, how come you boys ran out of the room without saying so much as hello?"

Sheepishly Mark said, "We're really sorry about your not being dead and everything. I mean if you *were* dead, we would have been sorry."

Afterward while the boys were sitting in the funeral parlor, sipping hot cocoa and wolfing down Mrs. Ellenberger's chocolate chip cookies, Mr. Ellenberger talked to them. In a serious voice he said, "You have to respect dead people, boys. You can't go paying for a peek. I know it was for a good cause. And since it wasn't really a body, you can keep the money. Just remember, in the future, leave dead people alone."

The boys promised they would. And they meant it.

7
It's Not the Same!

The following Thursday, right in the middle of a spelling test, Mr. Chickering's voice came over the loudspeaker. "Will the committee of fourth-grade girls who sold the candy at Blodget's Supermarket kindly come to my office?"

All the way down to the office the girls held hands. "What if we poisoned someone?" Theresa said.

"We'll be on *Court TV*," Stacey said.

"Would we all go to prison for life?" Bethany asked. "Or would they just divide a hundred years by four? Twenty-five years wouldn't be so bad."

When they walked into the principal's office, Mr. Chickering was smiling. Stacey decided it couldn't be fatal. "Well, girls, I have a letter for you." He handed it to Stacey. Everyone gathered around her and began to read:

Love'em Candy Company
3780 Sweet Street
Duck Creek, Ohio

Dear Starvation Lake Elementary Fourth-Grade Candy Committee:

Our salesman, Mr. Brookside, brought us a piece of candy you made. We were most impressed. Our firm is always on the lookout for new products. Can you furnish us with more samples of the product? If so, we might be willing to make you a substantial offer for your recipe. Mr. Brookside will pick up the samples at Blodget's Supermarket this Saturday afternoon.

Sincerely,
Donald Elker, Chairman

Mr. Chickering said in a hurt voice, "You didn't give me any of the candy." Then he became businesslike. "I suppose you have the recipe?"

"We know what we put into it," Stacey said. "Only we didn't exactly measure."

"I'm sure we can make it again," said Theresa.

The other girls all nodded. Dawn's moose's head bobbed up and down, too.

On their way back to the classroom,

they all talked at once. Even Dawn.

"We'll be rich," Stacey said.

"We'll be famous," Theresa said.

"We'll make a lot of money for the school," Bethany said.

"We could take a trip," Dawn said. "Downstate." They all knew the hospital Dawn's mother was in was downstate.

"And to California," Theresa said.

It was Stacey's idea to make the candy at Bethany's house. "Your mom's kitchen is so clean. When you have a business, inspectors come. Our kitchen would never pass." The other girls agreed.

Stacey slept over at Theresa's on Friday night. When she called home, she told Weird Mom they were making the candy at Bethany's.

"Why aren't you making it here?"

Weird Mom wanted to know. She sounded disappointed. Stacey mumbled something about Bethany's house being closer, what with the snow and all. She wouldn't have hurt her mom's feelings for anything.

Early Saturday morning, the girls gathered in the Conways' kitchen. The walls of the kitchen were a sunny yellow. The little squares of yellow linoleum were spotless. There wasn't a dirty dish in sight. Even the snow outside the Conways' windows seemed whiter than anywhere else.

On the counter, Mrs. Conway had placed a new package of marshmallows, an unopened tin of nuts, and several fresh bars of chocolate.

Mrs. Conway was neat and trim, like a small dog after a good brushing. She had aprons for all the girls, and she tied each one with a perky bow. "Everything is ready for you. I'll just get out of the way."

As soon as they were alone, they all looked at Dawn. "Tell us how to do it," Theresa said.

In a small voice, Dawn said, "Just like we did it before."

Bethany took a polished pan from the cupboard. It looked like it had never been used. She melted the fresh chocolate. The crisp nuts and plump marshmallows went into the chocolate. They poured the mixture onto a shiny platter and waited. When the candy was hard, they cut it up and wrapped up the pieces.

Stacey's dad drove them to Blodget's in his van. "Guess I'd better drive carefully," he said. He peered out the window as the windshield wipers swept away the snow.

"Looks like I've got valuable cargo here."

Stacey looked at Theresa. They smiled at each other. They were both thinking about being rich and famous.

When they thanked him for the ride, he laughed. "No problem. The missus is flying around the house like a bunch of lions are after her. I was glad to get out."

Mr. Brookside was waiting for them. He bounced up and down on his toes. "Well, girls, I can tell you our company's chairman, Mr. Elker, is pleased. He had some good things to say to me. Told me I knew how to keep my eyes and my mouth open, ha, ha. I see you've got the product." He snatched up a piece, unwrapped it, and popped it into his mouth.

The girls watched, holding their breath.

Mr. Brookside swallowed. He gave

them a puzzled look. "I guess I'll have one more," he said. This time he examined the collection of candy and slowly chose a piece. He carefully unwrapped it and put it into his mouth. Again the girls all held their breath and stared at Mr. Brookside.

He looked disappointed, even a little angry. "Some other candy company been at you girls? They offer you a lot of money? We can match their offer."

The girls all shook their heads.

"This isn't the same candy," he said. "Anyone can make candy like this."

The girls looked at one another. "Chocolate, nuts, and marshmallows," Bethany said, counting off on her fingers. "It's the same."

"We didn't do anything different," Theresa said. "Honest."

"And we haven't talked with any other company," Stacey said. "Could we try again?"

"Well, I've got to make about six more stops at stores around Desolation County. I could be back here in, say, two hours." He hurried off, pausing once to look suspiciously back at them.

"We did everything just like the last time," Stacey said.

Theresa thought for a minute. "Not exactly. The first time we made it at your house. This time we made it at Bethany's."

"What difference does that make?" Stacey asked. "The stuff we put into it was the same."

"The first time all the stuff was older," Theresa said. "And there was that gop in the pan."

They looked at one another. In a minute, they were flying out the door of Blodget's, trying not to run into the customers. Mr. Ward was scraping the snow from his windshield. "Dad," Stacey said, "could you take us home right away?"

"Sure, but I'd advise against it. Your ma is in a terrible mood today. I've never seen so much running around."

They all hurried up the Wards' snow-covered walk. Stacey led the way. The minute Stacey stuck her head into the house, she cried out, "It's the wrong house!"

Everyone stopped dead at the doorway. The old newspapers that were usually piled up on the floor were gone. The empty Coke bottles and dirty dishes had disappeared from the tables. Even the cat's kitty litter had been changed. In the

distance, Stacey heard a strange roaring sound. "What's that?" she asked, terrified.

"It's a vacuum cleaner," Bethany said.

The girls made a dash for the kitchen. The floor was spotless. The dirty dishes had vanished. The countertops shone. Weird Mom appeared with an old shirt tied around her waist like an apron.

"Mom! What did you do?" Stacey groaned.

Weird Mom smiled. "When I heard you were making the candy over at the Conways', I knew it was because our house was such a mess. I decided to clean things up. What do you think?"

"Have you got any old chocolate hidden away?" Stacey asked her mother.

"Cleared it all out."

"The marshmallows?" Dawn asked.

"Hard as rocks. Threw them away."

"What about the pan?" Theresa asked.

"Washed them all. I've been scrubbing all morning. Now you won't have to go someplace else to make your candy."

"But, Mom, that pan with the broken handle. Do you know what was in it?"

Weird Mom thought for a minute. "Maybe that was the pan I used to melt the candle wax. Or I might have made sweet and sour beets. Or boiled up the dye for my blouse. Or cooked the milk-weed pods. I'm sorry, dear, I just don't remember."

"Maybe the secret is where the house is located," Stacey said, without much hope. "You know, special vibrations or something. Anyhow, let's try. We haven't got anything to lose."

An hour later, Mr. Brookside tasted the second batch. "Worse than the first. You girls sure fooled me. I don't know what I'm going to tell Mr. Elker. He won't like it one bit. Too bad. You girls could have been rich and famous." He shook his head and started to walk out of Blodget's.

"Wait," Theresa called after him. "You didn't pay us for those three pieces you ate."

"You caused me a lot of trouble. I had to drive back here through all the snow."

"You caused us a lot of trouble, too."

He threw down two quarters. "Keep the change."

Mr. Gibbs had been watching from inside the store. Now he came out. "What are you going to do with all the candy you have left?"

They looked at one another and shrugged.

"I'll tell you what. I feel badly about what happened and I feel badly that it happened in my store. I'll buy the candy."

"What'll we do now?" Stacey asked, as they were walking away from the store.

Theresa said, "We could go over to your house and mess it up again."

8
Lights, Camera, Action

"Good morning, ladies and gentlemen. It's ten degrees outside and still snowing. However, we'll be going out for recess today. Also, I'm happy to announce that the fourth-grade boys collected fourteen dollars and the girls fourteen dollars and twenty cents toward the overnight." Stacey heard Mr. Chickering chew and swallow. It was his doughnut time.

"We have a TV crew here today. Over at the local station, they thought it might be a good idea if parents knew how the students are chipping in for the overnight at the ecology camp."

The reporter and a TV camera were already in the fourth-grade room. The reporter was Ralston Reger. He was shorter and older than he looked on TV and his hair was a little crooked. Ms. LaForest was wearing a black velvet skirt and a red velour sweater. She kept wetting her lips with her tongue and smiling. The camerawoman set up the lights.

Ralston told the fourth graders, "Now just forget the camera is here. Don't look at it. Look right at me as if you and I were just talking. Let's start with the boys. How did you fellows earn your money?"

No one said anything. They all shifted uncomfortably.

Ralston held the microphone up to Kevin. "Did you boys sell something?" he asked.

"Not exactly," Kevin said carefully. "It was more an educational thing. We gave the money to sort of learn something."

"Well, I'm impressed. Whose idea was this educational thing?"

The boys looked at Mark.

Ralston walked over and shoved the microphone in Mark's face. "Well, young man, would you care to describe for us exactly what you learned?"

Mark turned bright red. He opened his mouth, but nothing came out. He remembered his father's lecture. He knew his father would be plenty angry if the story appeared on TV.

Ralston gave him a sly smile. "You wouldn't be trying to hide anything?"

Mark's palms were sweaty. He wished the reporter would go away. He was scared one of the boys would blurt out the story.

Suddenly Baylor toppled over in his seat.

"I think he's fainted!" Tommy shouted. Everyone crowded around Baylor.

"Stand back, boys and girls. Give Baylor some air." Ms. LaForest explained to Ralston, "Baylor is a very delicate child. I think the excitement of the camera was too much for him. He's coming around now. Would you two help me get him down to the principal's office?"

As they half-lifted, half-dragged Baylor out of the room, he turned around and gave Mark a quick wink. Then he went limp again.

The minute the grown-ups left the room with Baylor, Tommy said, "He didn't

faint at all! He was just putting them on."

"Yeah, Mark," Kevin said, "he did it to get you off the spot."

Mark nodded. "Awesome."

Before the girls could find out what was going on, Ms. LaForest was back with Ralston and the camerawoman. "Time's running out," Ralston said. "Let's try the girls. What did you do to raise money?"

"We sold candy," Theresa said.

"And whose idea was that?"

The girls looked at Dawn. "Dawn, dear," Ms. LaForest said gently, "move your moose over. We can't see your face. Stacey, maybe you'd better tell the story." She turned to Ralston. "Dawn is a little shy."

But Dawn had already begun talking. "We didn't want to bake," she said, "so we decided to make candy. I know how. We all went to Stacey's house on Friday afternoon at about four o'clock. It was snowing outside...."

Dawn told the whole story. Ralston tried to hurry her past the details, but she wouldn't skip anything. It was as if she had stored up words for a whole year. Now they were all tumbling out. The whole class, including Ms. LaForest, stared at her. Fifteen minutes later, and long after the camera had been turned off, Dawn finished, "...so Mr. Gibbs bought the rest of the candy."

Ralston stared at her. "Well, young lady, I guess you have a future as a TV reporter. You sure know how to tell a tale. Unfortunately, we'll only have a few minutes in which to show the segment. We'll probably have to cut a little. Maybe the part about your friend's house. It's a great story, though. Be sure to watch tonight, kids. You'll be famous."

After school, the fourth graders walked through the blowing snow to the bus. Elvera cranked open the door. Usually they all crowded in, shoving in front of one another. Today the boys stood aside to let Baylor on first. Mark settled in next to him. Baylor shifted closer to the window.

"You don't have to worry about me having germs," Mark told Baylor. "They keep everything at the funeral parlor really clean."

Baylor seemed uncertain. "But you get people who died. They must have germs."

Mark gave him a patient look. "When a person dies, his germs die with him."

"Dawn," Stacey called across the aisle, "don't you want to come over here and sit next to me?"

Dawn shook her head. "The moose likes a window seat to himself." She pulled the moose close and looked out the window.

Suddenly Elvera stopped the bus and pulled over. They weren't anywhere near a regular stop. The bus got quiet. Everyone looked at Elvera to see what was wrong.

Elvera undid the flaps of her hunting cap and threw it up in the air. "Kids! Look out the window! It's stopped snowing!"

About the Author

While she was writing *Rich and Famous in Starvation Lake*, Gloria Whelan couldn't help thinking about her own home in northern Michigan. "My kitchen doesn't look exactly like Weird Mom's, but I have found a dried mouse or two," she says. "And that's nothing compared to the time a snake got in our washing machine!"

Gloria Whelan, the winner of the 2000 National Book Award for Young People's Literature, is known for writing well-crafted historical fiction. Some of her other books include *Once on This Island*, *Homeless Bird*, and the first book about the kids of Starvation Lake Elementary School, *Welcome to Starvation Lake*.